WICKEDLY CLEVER ANIMAL DEFENSES

REBECCA L. JOHNSON

M MILLBROOK PRESS . MINNEAPOLIS

For Bob and Tom

Millbrook Press
A division of Lerner Publishing Group, Inc.
241 First Avenue North
Minneapolis, MN 55401 USA

For reading levels and more information, look up this title at www.lernerbooks.com.

Main body text set in Avenir LT Std 13/20.
Typeface provided by Adobe Systems.

Library of Congress Cataloging-in-Publication Data

Johnson, Rebecca L.
When lunch fights back : wickedly clever animal defenses / by Rebecca L. Johnson.
pages cm
Includes bibliographical references and index.
ISBN 978–1–4677–2109–7 (lib. bdg. : alk. paper)
ISBN 978–1–4677–4766–0 (eBook)
1. Animal defenses—Juvenile literature. I. Title.
QL759.J64 2015
591.47—dc23 2013046646

Manufactured in the United States of America
1 – DP – 7/15/14

CONTENTS

INTRODUCTION

THE CHALLENGE OF SURVIVAL

No one said living on planet Xenon would be easy. Hungry aliens are everywhere. A new group just slithered into view. The aliens are well-armed with lasers and a contraption that shoots out nets for capturing prey.

THE PREY, OF COURSE, IS YOU.

You roll your shoulders and grip the video game controls. Thumbs poised over the buttons, you're ready to defend yourself with weapons of your own. You're not going down without a fight.

Win or lose, though, the battle on planet Xenon is just a game.

Not so here on planet Earth. On Earth the challenge of survival is a real and serious business. In the wild, every living thing is constantly at risk of being eaten by something else. Good defenses can mean the difference between surviving a predator's attack and becoming its lunch.

Sharp teeth and claws are common defensive weapons among Earth's animals. So are clever camouflage and being very, very good at hiding. And don't forget speed, for fast getaways. But if you think that's the best nature can do, be prepared to be surprised.

Good defenses can mean the difference between life and death.

CHAPTER 1

SLIP-SLIMING AWAY

ATLANTIC HAGFISH

Scientific name: *Myxine glutinosa* (MIK-sih-nee gloo-tih-NOH-suh)

Distribution: Atlantic Ocean

Habitat: on or near the ocean bottom

Size: up to 2.5 feet (0.76 meters) long

A hagfish rests on the muddy ocean bottom.

A hagfish slithers along the ocean bottom, moving like a snake. This primitive deep-sea creature is nearly blind but has a keen sense of smell. It picked up the scent of a dead whale from more than 1 mile (1.6 kilometers) away.

The hagfish follows the smell through the water. When it reaches the whale's carcass, it swims around the remains, sizing up the feast. Then the hagfish sinks its teeth into the dead whale's soft, rotting flesh and takes a big bite.

As the hagfish eats, a shark arrives. The shark isn't interested in the whale, though. It's after fresh meat. Slowly circling, the shark edges closer to the hagfish until it is just inches away. In a blur of movement, the shark strikes. It grabs the hagfish in its toothy jaws—and instantly lets go. The shark's mouth is overflowing with thick, snot-like goo. The slimy stuff fills its throat and clogs its gills. Without gills to pull oxygen from the water, the shark can't breathe. It thrashes its head from side to side with jerky, desperate movements.

Unharmed, the hagfish pays no attention. Strings of slime still ooze from its long rubbery body as it goes back to eating.

The shark convulses with what looks like a gigantic cough. Clouds of slime billow out from its gills and throat. Finally able to breathe again, the shark darts away without a backward glance.

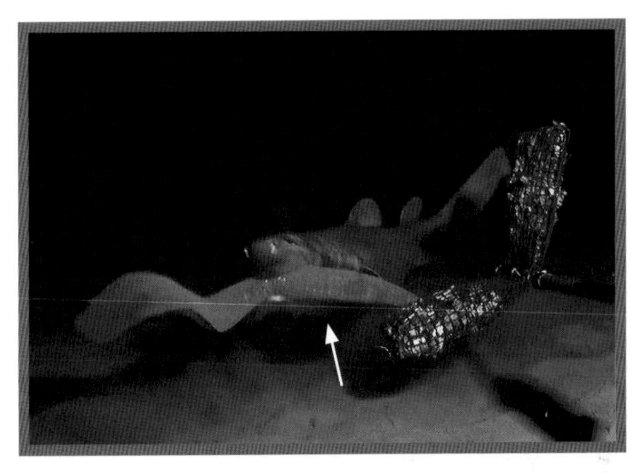

New Zealand scientists captured these photos of a shark attacking a hagfish. The arrows show the cloud of slime the hagfish released.

THE SCIENCE BEHIND THE STORY

Hagfish aren't fish, despite their name. They are primitive eel-like animals that have been roaming the ocean for millions of years. Hagfish have no jaws and no backbone. What they do have, however, is slime. Douglas Fudge should know.

Fudge is a biologist at the University of Guelph in Ontario, Canada. He has been studying hagfish and their slimy defense since 1997. "The slime is amazingly effective at preventing hagfish from being eaten by fish predators, including sharks," said Fudge. Hagfish release slime the moment something tries to bite them—or even just bothers them. Fudge has been "slimed" many times while gently handling hagfish in his laboratory.

The slime comes from special glands in the hagfish's skin. The glands actually release two ingredients that combine to make the slime. One ingredient is slippery mucus. The other is threadlike fibers. "Hagfish slime is the only slime we know of [in nature] that has fibers," Fudge explained.

When a predator such as a shark bites a hagfish, a lot happens in a short time. Mucus is ejected from the glands as tiny little packages. Fibers are ejected as coiled threads. The mucus swells, and the fibers uncoil the moment they contact seawater. "The fibers and the mucus together form an intricate network that is very good at trapping water," said Fudge.

The result is a mixture that expands tremendously—and incredibly rapidly. "It all happens in about 100 milliseconds, or a tenth of a second," said Fudge. In other words, hagfish make great gobs of slime in the blink of an eye. It's a nearly unbeatable defense.

Hagfish are nicknamed snot eels for good reason: they can release handfuls of slippery slime in seconds.

CHAPTER 2

CONCEALED WEAPONS

A hairy frog's toe pads help it cling to surfaces and also conceal its defensive weapons.

AFRICAN HAIRY FROG

Scientific name: *Trichobatrachus robustus* (trik-oh-buh-TRAK-uhs row-BUHS-tuhs)

Distribution: western Africa, primarily from Cameroon to Democratic Republic of the Congo

Habitat: fast-flowing rivers in lowland rain forests

Size: 4.5 inches (11 centimeters)

An African hairy frog sits in the leaves beside a rushing river. A moment ago, the grass along the riverbank moved ever so slightly. Instinctively, the frog froze.

A river otter crouches in the grass. Muscles tensed, it watches the frog and waits for it to get closer. Eventually the frog relaxes and starts climbing up the bank. The otter springs and catches the frog by one of its front legs.

Without teeth or claws, the African hairy frog seems defenseless. But as it kicks out with its hind legs, it unleashes hidden weapons. Pointed bits of bone poke out through the pads on its rear toes.

The frog uses the sharp bones like claws. It rakes them across the otter's sensitive nose. Surprised, the otter loosens its grip. The frog wrenches free and leaps into the river's fast-moving current.

African clawless otters eat many kinds of small animals, including fish and frogs. It's likely that these otters try to eat hairy frogs, although scientists have never caught one in the act.

The sharp tips of a hairy frog's "bone claws" poke through the skin on its rear toes.

THE SCIENCE BEHIND THE STORY

Many vertebrate animals have claws. A typical claw grows from the end of an animal's toe. It sticks out beyond the toe's tip and is made of a hard material called keratin. That same material makes up your fingernails.

The African hairy frog doesn't have claws—at least not typical ones. When threatened, however, it creates effective substitutes. Biologist David Blackburn and his colleagues at Harvard University figured out how the hairy frog deploys its unusual weapons. Blackburn, now an assistant curator at the California Academy of Sciences, used dissections and X-rays to peer inside the frog's hind feet.

Blackburn discovered that the last bone in each of the hairy frog's rear toes is pointed and curved. It's shaped like a cat's claw. "Just beyond this curved bone is a small bony nodule," Blackburn said. "The curved bone is connected to the bony nodule by a piece of tough tissue."

Attached to the other end of the curved bone is a muscle. "When the muscle contracts, it breaks the connection between the bone and the bony nodule and releases the curved, claw-like bone," Blackburn explained. The contracting muscle pulls the curved bone down through the frog's toe. The bone's pointed end pokes through the skin of the toe pad, and—*presto*—an instant claw!

"If you pick up a nice big hairy frog, the first thing it does is kick its feet and rake its claws against your skin," said Blackburn. How sharp are these claws? "They're like the points of really sharp pencils and can certainly give you a good bloody scratch."

When danger passes, the hairy frog retracts its bony weapons. The punctures in its toe pads may heal. But inside the toes, the claws are still there, ready for action.

A view inside the toe of a hairy frog reveals the curved bone that breaks free from the small bony nodule and drops down to form a claw.

The orange markings along the sides of a Spanish ribbed newt are where its sharp-tipped ribs will emerge from its skin.

SPANISH RIBBED NEWT

Scientific name: *Pleurodeles waltl* (pler-oh-DEE-leez WALL-tuhl)

Distribution: Spain, Portugal, and northern Morocco

Habitat: small deep ponds, lakes, and slow-moving streams

Size: up to 12 inches (30 cm)

ANOTHER BONY BREAKTHROUGH

The Spanish ribbed newt also uses bones as weapons but in a very different way. When threatened, it forces the tips of its ribs through the sides of its body. This creates two rows of needle-sharp spines.

Zoologist Egon Heiss from Austria's University of Vienna has studied the newt, which is a type of salamander. When threatened by predators such as foxes and ferrets, many salamanders flare their ribs to make their bodies look bigger.

Spanish ribbed newts, however, have extraordinary ribs. "Their ribs are much longer compared to other salamanders and sharply pointed at the tips," explained Heiss. When the newt flares its ribs, their sharp tips press hard against the animal's body wall. So hard, in fact, that they tear right through and poke out of the skin.

The Spanish ribbed newt also produces a milky white poison from glands in its skin. It is truly nasty stuff. "If the skin secretion touches an animal's eyes or mouth, it burns like red hot chili—I know from experience!" Heiss said. "But if it gets into an animal's bloodstream, it can be deadly, even in small amounts."

As the newt's ribs poke out through its skin, the sharp tips become coated with poison. If a predator catches a newt and bites down hard, it gets more than a mouthful of pain. The newt's rib tips act like hypodermic needles, injecting poison deep into the tissues lining the predator's mouth.

Spanish ribbed newts may survive most predator attacks—even if the predators don't. When all the fuss is over, the newts simply pull their ribs back inside their bodies. The holes made by the rib tips heal remarkably quickly, leaving the newts as good as new.

You can see the poisoned tips of the newt's ribs sticking out of its side in this photo.

CHAPTER 3 TOXIC BUBBLES

A blue-spotted *N. taracua* termite (arrow) mingles with other workers and a soldier (the termite with the huge head).

NEOCAPRITERMES TARACUA TERMITES

Scientific name: *Neocapritermes taracua* (nee-oh-kap-PRIH-tur-meez tah-RAK-you-uh)

Distribution: French Guiana

Habitat: rain forest

Size: about 0.4 inch (1 cm) long

The old termite shuffles through the nest. Younger workers push past her. They are faster and stronger. They can cut wood—termite food—so easily with their sharp mandibles. The old termite's mandibles are almost too dull to cut anything anymore. Still, she has something her younger nest mates do not: two blue spots that gleam on her back.

Suddenly there's a commotion at the nest entrance. The colony is under attack by an enemy termite species. The old termite hurries out to help defend her home. Colony soldiers bite attackers in half, but they can only kill one enemy at a time.

The old termite wades into the battle. Half a dozen invaders rush toward her. She nips at them with her dull mandibles, but they quickly overpower her. She waits until she is covered with enemies. Then she triggers the blue-spotted weapon on her back.

A drop of liquid gushes out of her ruptured body. The enemies that had been clinging to her twitch and die. Sadly, so does the old termite. But she sacrifices herself to help her colony survive.

Under attack by two enemy termites, a blue-spotted *N. taracua* (*center*) deploys her chemical weapon, releasing a deadly drop of toxin (*arrow*).

THE SCIENCE BEHIND THE STORY

While slogging through a rain forest in French Guiana, scientists Thomas Bourguignon and Jan Sobotnik came upon a colony of *N. taracua* termites. They noticed something odd as they watched the insects go in and out of their nest. Some termite workers had blue spots on their backs. Intrigued, Bourguignon grabbed one with a forceps. The termite promptly burst.

Very carefully, the scientists collected several blue-spotted workers and examined them more closely. The blue spots, they discovered, were tiny pouches filled with blue crystals. "We exported [some of the] termites to our lab in the Czech Republic, where a team of biochemists analyzed them," explained Bourguignon. The crystals turned out to be a copper-containing protein. Related proteins are secreted in termite digestive tracts. But no one had ever seen pouches full of this protein on a termite's back.

The cluster of blue crystals in one side of a *N. taracua*'s explosive "backpack" is magnified about two hundred times in this photo taken with a scanning electron microscope.

Obviously, the crystal-filled pouches were some sort of defensive weapon. But how did it work? The scientists dissected a blue-spotted worker under a microscope. Beneath her crystal-filled pouches, they discovered a set of salivary glands.

Mixing saliva from these glands with some of the blue crystals instantly forms a toxic liquid. The scientists suspect that when blue-spotted workers are attacked, they somehow break open their crystal-filled pouches and the underlying salivary glands. Crystals and saliva combine, forming a drop of toxic liquid that bubbles up out of the termite's back.

"Obviously, *N. taracua* workers avoid triggering the mixing of the blue crystals and saliva, as this causes their death," said Bourguignon. "However, when they are bitten by an enemy, then they trigger their weapon. This self-sacrifice is the last chance for *N. taracua* workers to harm their enemies."

It's a very effective sacrifice. Every enemy within range drops dead.

CHAPTER 4

MASTER BLASTERS

Hoopoe chicks rest in their nest.

Scientific name: *Upupa epops* (oo-POO-pah EE-pohps)

Distribution: Africa, Europe, Middle East, and much of Asia

Habitat: dry woodlands, orchards, and city suburbs

Size: 10 to 12 inches (25 to 31 cm) long, with 18-inch (46 cm) wingspan.

The hoopoe chicks snuggle together in their nest inside a hollow tree. They're only a few days old. It will be weeks before they can fly. In the forest outside, the chicks can hear their parents softly calling. *Hoop-hoop-hoop*. The parent birds repeat the call again and again as they gather insects for their chicks to eat.

A moment later, the chicks hear something else: the *scritch-scratching* of sharp claws on tree bark. Something is climbing their tree. Suddenly the parents are loudly *HOOP-HOOP-HOOP*ing. The chicks hear an angry flutter of wings followed by a snarl and a hiss.

The parent hoopoes keep up the attack but to no avail. A dark shape appears at the nest entrance. Green eyes framed by long whiskers peer in at the chicks. It's a cat on the prowl for lunch.

The chicks are ready, though. They know instinctively what to do. All together, they turn their backs toward the intruder. The chicks lean forward, lift their tiny rumps, and shoot streams of foul-smelling feces directly into the cat's face. There's a howl and a screech. The cat hits the ground running, trying desperately to escape the incredible stench.

Hoopoe chicks seem like an easy meal until predators experience their smelly defense firsthand.

While hoopoe chicks defend themselves with streams of stinky poop, their parents fight off predators with sharp beaks and strong wings.

THE SCIENCE BEHIND THE STORY

The hoopoe is a pigeon-sized bird with a flashy crest of feathers. It's famous for its revolting, smelly defense. Hoopoe chicks can fire reeking streams of feces more than 18 inches (46 cm) with deadly accuracy. Getting plastered with hoopoe poop is enough to drive away even the most determined predator.

Scientists wondered why hoopoe feces smell so terrible. They discovered that hoopoes have an oil-producing gland just under their tail. The gland contains an unusual mix of smelly chemical compounds. Some of these chemicals are produced by the gland. Others, however, are produced by bacteria that live inside it!

THE FULMAR'S FLIPSIDE

A fulmar chick sits alone on a rocky ledge high on a windswept cliff. One wrong step and it could easily fall. It would plunge to its death in the cold ocean far below since it's not yet able to fly. So the chick is careful. It simply sits, hardly moving, waiting for its parents to return. They are catching fish far out at sea.

Other birds, however, are looking for food closer to home. A broad-winged skua soars past the cliff. Skuas eat mostly fish. But given a chance, they will gobble up the chicks of almost any other bird.

A fulmar chick sits alone on the rock ledge that serves as its nest.

FULMAR

Scientific name: *Fulmarus glacialis* (fuhl-MAY-ruhs glay-see-AY-lihs)

Distribution: northern Atlantic Ocean, and parts of Arctic and northern Pacific Oceans

Habitat: ocean; nests on steep, rocky, sea cliffs

Size: 16 to 20 inches (40 to 50 cm), with 40- to 44-inch (102 to 112 cm) wingspan

A skua will attack almost any defenseless chick.

The skua swoops in and lands on the ledge. It sizes up the chick with black, beady eyes. The chick seems to shrink into itself and gives out a faint chirp. Emboldened, the skua steps closer. It takes first one step, then two. A third step brings it within range.

The fulmar chick opens its mouth wide, as if it's going to scream. But it isn't sound that comes out of the chick's mouth. A stream of putrid, orange-yellow vomit erupts from its throat and sails through the air. The foul-smelling stinky stuff hits the skua hard, splattering all over one wing. The skua takes off, surprised and alarmed. It has no idea its days may be numbered.

A fulmar's long, ropy stream of vomit makes a very effective defensive weapon. Adult fulmars, as well as chicks, can fend off predators this way.

THE SCIENCE BEHIND THE STORY

The word *fulmar* means "foul gull." The name refers to fulmar chicks' horrid, fishy-smelling vomit, which they spew onto anything that threatens them. A fulmar chick can hit a moving target up to 6 feet (2 m) away. It can also hurl out half a dozen blasts of vomit in quick succession. Scientists have discovered that fulmar chicks can even defend themselves with vomit while hatching, before they are completely free of their shells!

Fulmar vomit is mostly a mixture of oily substances secreted by the bird's stomach wall. It has a vile odor and is as sticky as glue. Once the vomit gets on another bird's feathers, no amount of cleaning and preening will remove it.

In studying the effects of fulmar vomit on bird feathers, scientists were surprised to discover it can be a potentially deadly defensive weapon. Chemicals in the oil gradually destroy the waterproof coating on the feathers of many types of birds. Without the coating, feathers become matted, waterlogged, and useless. When seabirds whose feathers are contaminated with fulmar chick vomit land on the ocean's surface, they may not be able to take off again. Eventually, they'll drown.

Fortunately for fulmars, they are "immune" to their own vomit. Scientists can't explain why, but fulmars can clean off the oily stuff and their feathers suffer no ill effects. This means that parent fulmars don't have to worry while their chicks are perfecting their aim.

CHAPTER 5

KNOCKOUT PUNCH

PEACOCK MANTIS SHRIMP

Scientific name: *Odontodactylus scyllarus* (oh-dohn-toh-DAK-tih-luhs sih-LAY-ruhs)

Distribution: Indian and western Pacific Oceans

Habitat: sandy and gravelly ocean bottom, often near coral reefs

Size: 1 to 7 inches (3 to 18 cm)

Decked out in rainbow colors, a peacock mantis shrimp looks fairly harmless at first glance.

Two bulging pink eyes sit atop neon-blue stalks. The eyes belong to a peacock mantis shrimp that is crouched in its small rocky den. The mantis shrimp holds its large forelimbs high and close to its body. The rounded hammers at the "elbows" of the forelimbs are cocked and ready.

The eyes swivel left, right, up and down, as the mantis shrimp scans its surroundings for movement. Movement often means food. Something slithers around a nearby rock. The mantis shrimp scoots forward to get a better look. This something is not food, however. It's the tip of an arm. A long, suckered arm attached to a big octopus.

The whole octopus slides into view. It spots the mantis shrimp and moves closer. The mantis shrimp is much smaller than the octopus. Yet it stands its ground. It waits and watches the bigger predator with its nonstop eyes.

The octopus shoots out an arm and makes a grab for the mantis shrimp. *BAM!* The mantis shrimp retaliates with an underhand blow. The hammers on its forelimbs move incredibly fast. They strike tender octopus flesh with tremendous force.

The octopus jerks back. The mantis shrimp scoots forward and strikes out again—*WHAM!* The octopus draws in its arms and flushes dark red. It is no match for the mantis shrimp's knockout punch. Defeated, it slithers away.

Octopuses eat mostly small fish and crustaceans, including lobsters, shrimp, and . . . mantis shrimp. Nevertheless, mantis shrimp often successfully chase away octopuses many times their size.

THE SCIENCE BEHIND THE STORY

Mantis shrimp are cousins of lobsters and shrimp. There are many different mantis shrimp species, and most would fit on the palm of your hand. But you probably wouldn't want to hold one. Mantis shrimp are ferocious predators armed with unique and powerful weapons.

The weapons are the forelimbs, of course. They come in two varieties. Spearer-type mantis shrimp have spine-studded forelimbs that open and close like a bear trap. Smasher-types, like the peacock mantis shrimp, have forearms equipped with rounded, club-like elbows. They use these hammers for smashing the hard shells of snails, crabs, and clams. Once the shells have been broken open, the mantis shrimp devours the soft flesh inside.

A peacock mantis shrimp keeps its powerful hammers tucked away (*arrow*) until it is ready to use them.

What works for killing prey also helps the mantis shrimp defend itself against predators. When it feels threatened, it lashes out with astonishing speed and force. Just how fast can a smasher-type mantis shrimp deliver its punch? That's what biologist Sheila Patek wanted to know. Working at the University of California at Berkeley, Patek and fellow biologist Roy Caldwell used high-speed cameras to film peacock mantis shrimp striking out with their hammers.

When the scientists viewed the film in slow motion, they were able to calculate the speed at which the hammers move. And the answer is . . . about 50 miles per hour, or 23 meters per second! A single punch takes just 1.8 milliseconds to occur. Imagine pumping your fists that fast—underwater! The peacock mantis shrimp's hammer strike is one of the fastest known movements made by living things in the ocean.

A peacock mantis shrimp's punch isn't just fast. It's so powerful it can crack the rock-hard shells of snails and other animals the mantis shrimp eats. Working at Duke University, Patek designed experiments to measure the power of that punch. She tricked a mantis shrimp living in an aquarium into punching an instrument that measures the force of a blow. The technical term is *impact force*.

Patek recorded mantis shrimp punches again and again. She could hardly believe the results. The mantis shrimp typically struck the instrument with well over 200 pounds (890 newtons) of force. "The hammer impact is massive," she says. "These animals are producing thousands of times their body weight in peak impact force. As far as I know this still holds the record as the highest force generation of any organism that has been measured on the planet."

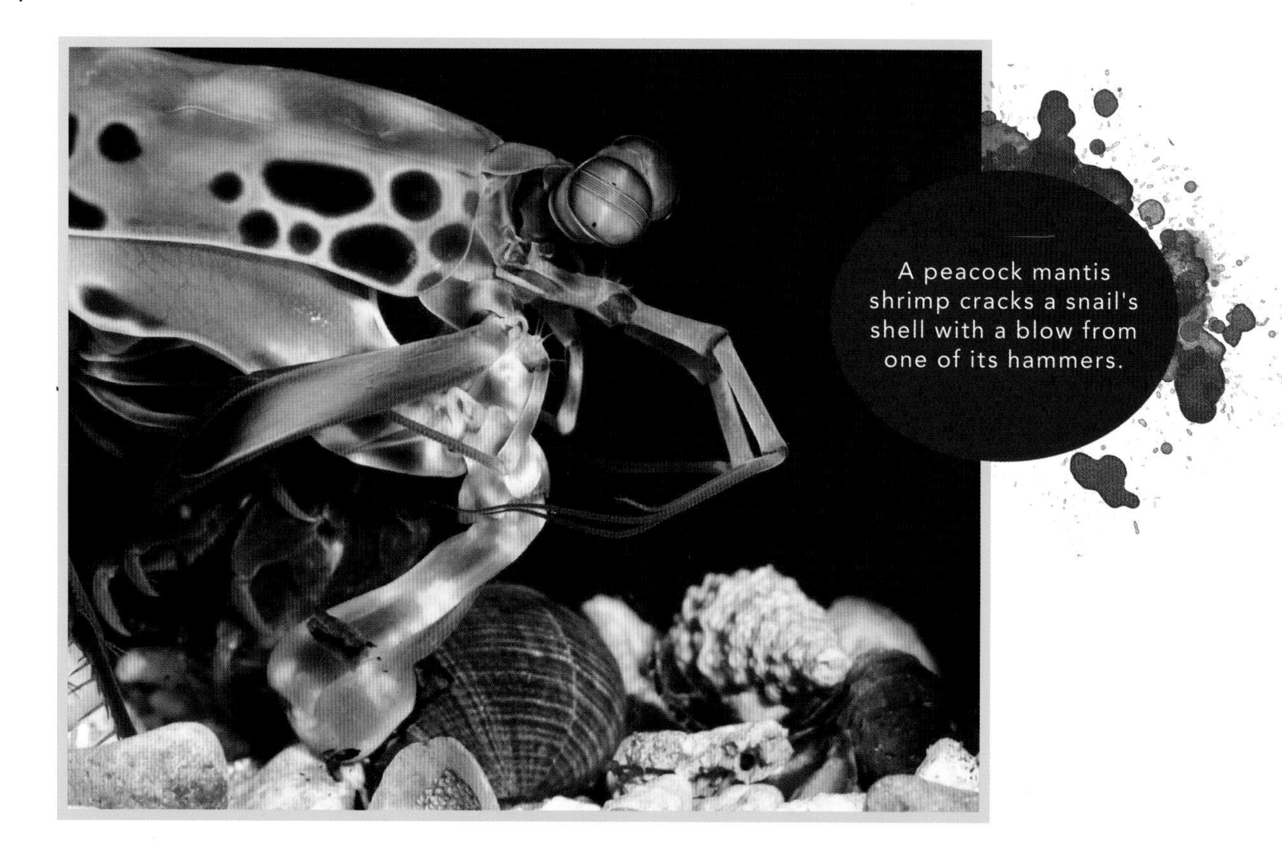

A peacock mantis shrimp cracks a snail's shell with a blow from one of its hammers.

Rows of aquariums are home to mantis shrimp in Sheila's Patek's lab at Duke University (*left*). The glass wall of an aquarium in Roy Caldwell's lab shatters as a peacock mantis shrimp delivers a powerful punch (*below*).

Patek has been punched by different species of mantis shrimp quite a few times. What does it feel like? "Being punched is not so bad. It feels a little like a beesting," she said. Rows of aquariums line Patek's laboratory. They are home to dozens of smasher-type mantis shrimp that technically can hit hard enough to break glass. "I've never had any mantis shrimp break our [aquariums]," Patek admitted. "They don't normally strike the glass unless provoked, so obviously we try to avoid that behavior."

In other words, in Patek's lab full of mantis shrimp, nobody taps on the glass.

CHAPTER 6
HERE'S BLOOD IN YOUR EYE

Spots, stripes, and earth-tone colors help horned lizards blend into dry, rocky ground.

TEXAS HORNED LIZARD

Scientific name: *Phrynosoma cornutum* (frih-NOH-suh-muh kohr-NOO-tuhm)

Distribution: Texas, New Mexico, Oklahoma, Kansas, Colorado, and northern Mexico

Habitat: dry scrubby grasslands

Size: 2.5 to 4.5 inches (6.4 to 11 cm), not including tail

A horned lizard basks beneath the hot Texas sun. It rests in a dry gully, digesting a bellyful of ants. The only sounds are the rustle of wind through the grass and a distant hawk's cry. But the lizard feels something. A slight tremor runs through the ground. Something is coming. Something big enough to be a threat.

The lizard sees the coyote as it crests the hill and trots down into the gully. Like a balloon deflating, the lizard flattens itself against the ground. The knobs and spines on its scaly skin blend with the rocks that surround it. The horns on its head even cast small shadows, breaking up the lizard's outline. It's perfect camouflage.

But perfect camouflage is not enough. The coyote has keen eyesight and a superb sense of smell. It catches the lizard's scent and stalks over to investigate.

Knowing it's been discovered, the lizard tries to look big and fierce. It spreads out its spine-rimmed back to make its body seem wider. It brandishes the horns on its head. But the coyote isn't put off. Snarling, it bares its teeth to bite.

The horned lizard resorts to its secret weapon. It tenses its muscles and arches its back. It closes its eyes as the eyelids seem to swell. Suddenly, a thin stream of blood shoots out of the lizard's right eye. It rockets through the air like a jet of water fired from a squirt gun. The blood hits the coyote right in the mouth. The coyote makes a face and shakes it head, trying to get rid of the blood. The lizard sees its chance to escape. It darts over to a low rock ledge and squeezes beneath it, beyond the reach of the coyote's teeth and claws.

A coyote that attacks a horned lizard is in for a bloody, bad-tasting surprise.

THE SCIENCE BEHIND THE STORY

If you want to know something about horned lizards, ask Wade Sherbrooke. A biologist with the American Museum of Natural History, Sherbrooke is a world expert on horned lizards and their blood-squirting defense. He's spent years figuring out how it works.

When a horned lizard is threatened, it tightens certain muscles in its head. The muscles squeeze on large veins, restricting the blood's movement. Blood can flow into the lizard's head, but it can't flow out. As blood accumulates in the lizard's head, the pressure inside blood vessels builds. Eventually, tiny blood vessels in tissues around one of the lizard's eyes rupture. Blood suddenly comes squirting out from around the lower edge of the eye, through the tear duct.

Scientists aren't sure if all species of horned lizards can shoot blood from their eyes. Those that do, however, can put on an impressive show. They may alternate eyes, shooting first from one and then the other. And the amount of blood they let loose can be substantial. In one set of

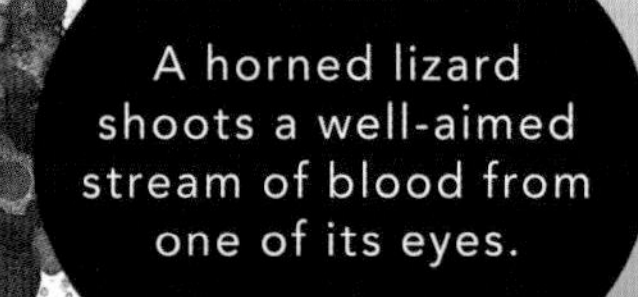

A horned lizard shoots a well-aimed stream of blood from one of its eyes.

experiments, Sherbrooke and his colleague George Middendorf found that some horned lizards, when threatened repeatedly, squirted out more than half the blood in their bodies—and they survived just fine. "We don't think that the lizards use this much blood defensively, in the wild," Sherbrooke said. He suspects that most horned lizards use only a few squirts.

Interestingly, horned lizards tend to reserve their bloody weapon for members of the dog and cat families. The reason? The taste of horned lizard blood is something dogs, foxes, coyotes, bobcats, and their relatives apparently can't stand. "In our experiments, we've demonstrated that horned lizard blood contains compounds that are distasteful to canids and felids [dog and cat family members]," Sherbrooke explained. In order to be effective, a horned lizard's bloody defense must be accurately aimed. "The blood needs to hit receptors in the mouth." For horned lizards, that means their aim has to be deadly, or they'll likely end up dead.

Blood released from a horned lizard's eye is under so much pressure that it can travel many feet through the air.

CHAPTER 7

OF BULLIES AND BAIT

Two-spot astyanax get their name from the pairs of dark spots on their pale bodies.

TWO-SPOT ASTYANAX

Scientific name: *Astyanax bimaculatus* (ah-STY-ah-naks by-mak-you-LAY-tuhs)

Distribution: most of South America

Habitat: small streams, ponds, and rivers

Size: about 6 inches (15 cm)

Small silvery fish move slowly along with the lazy current. They are two-spot astyanax, common in Brazilian rivers and streams. The two-spots stay together in a group, or school, as they nibble on river bottom plants. Little fish in a school have a better chance of surviving when a predator attacks. There is safety in numbers, you know.

At least, that's how it usually works.

A large, streamlined fish suddenly appears, moving fast toward the two-spot school. It's a wolf fish with a low-slung bottom jaw and rows of pointed teeth. The two-spots see the predator coming toward them at full speed.

Without warning, one member of the two-spot school turns on its closest neighbor and bites him viciously. A few other bullies join in. They push and shove the injured fish out of the school. He tries desperately to swim back into the group. But his schoolmates won't let him. Alone in the water, he's completely exposed. He is the victim. The target. The bait.

The wolf fish strikes. In one quick gulp, the injured two-spot is gone. Satisfied, the big fish swims away. The two-spot school relaxes and goes back to nibbling. For the moment, they are safe. If the predator returns, though, they will be ready. They won't hesitate to turn on another member of their group and offer it up as a sacrifice.

A wolf fish won't hesitate to gobble up an injured two-spot that is outside the school.

THE SCIENCE BEHIND THE STORY

Biologist Robert Young studies animal behavior. When he started working with two-spot astyanax in Brazil, his goal was to help protect them from a human-made danger. Two-spots are common in rivers throughout South America, including rivers with hydroelectric power plants. Two-spots often swim into power plant turbines. It's a fatal mistake, because the turbine's spinning blades can kill the fish. Young wanted to devise a way to keep the two-spots out of the turbines. He wondered if scaring the little fish away with models of predators might be a solution.

In his laboratory at the University of Salford in Britain, Young and his student Vinicius Goulart set up eight large aquariums. They put a small school of two-spots into each one. They made realistic models of two-spot predators, including wolf fish. Then they designed experiments to see how the little fish responded to different sorts of predator attacks.

What happened next was completely unexpected. "When he first started the experiments, Vin came running out of the lab to find me," Young recalled. "He said, 'Rob, something weird is going on with these fish.'"

Goulart used the wolf-fish model like a puppet in the water. Whenever he "chased" two-spots with the model, the little fish turned on one member of their group. They bit it and forced it out of the school. "The injured fish would swim away from the school for several centimeters

Two-spot astyanax gather in schools of up to fifty individuals in their natural habitats.

and then try to get back in," Young explained. Eventually it did—in the aquariums. In the wild, however, the scientists guessed it would have been quickly eaten.

An injured two-spot is tempting for two reasons. First, it is alone. Second, when two-spots (and many other fish) are injured, cells in their skin release a chemical. The chemical acts like an alarm to warn other fish of danger. Any fish producing this chemical, however, is usually targeted by predators as an easy meal.

What two-spots do when attacked by predators is the first scientifically documented case of what Young calls "active selfish behavior" in nature. In other words, animals deliberately sacrifice one individual so the rest of the group can survive. It seems underhanded. Nasty. Even cruel. But Young cautions against thinking about two-spots this way. "As humans, we consider the consequences of our actions. Animals don't. They simply act in the way that evolution has shaped them to act."

CHAPTER 8
MEET MY BODYGUARDS

The mustard plants in this field are blooming—and also under attack.

BLACK MUSTARD

Scientific name: *Brassica nigra* (BRASS-ik-uh NY-gruh)

Distribution: Europe, North Africa, Middle East, southwest Asia, and parts of India

Habitat: cultivated as a crop and grows wild as a weed

Size: up to 6.6 feet (2 m) high

A field of black mustard plants is in bloom. The plants' dainty yellow flowers attract honeybees and other insect pollinators. The flowers also attract hordes of large cabbage white butterflies. Actually, the butterflies are more interested in the plants' leaves than their flowers. That's because the butterfly *caterpillars* like to eat them.

All over the field, the butterflies begin laying eggs. Each female butterfly lays her eggs in tidy rows on mustard plant leaves. In a few days, small yellow caterpillars will emerge from the eggs. They will start *munch-munch-munch*ing the leaves. The more caterpillars that hatch, the more leaves the mustard plants will lose.

That's why the mustard plants are fighting back. They're calling in their bodyguards.

PARASITOID WASP
TRICHOGRAMMA BRASSICAE

Scientific name: *Trichogramma brassicae* (trik-oh-GRAM-uh BRASS-ik-ee)

Distribution: Europe

Habitat: croplands and woodlands

Size: 0.012 to 0.016 inch (0.3 to 0.4 millimeters)

A tiny *T. brassicae* wasp lays her egg inside the egg of a large cabbage white butterfly.

Cells in the mustard plant leaves produce special chemicals within hours of the egg laying. The chemicals pass out of the leaves and are carried away on the breeze. When certain tiny wasps get a whiff of these chemicals, they track them to their source. The wasps find the mustard plants—and the butterfly eggs on their leaves.

The wasps get to work quickly. Each female wasp spears one butterfly egg after another with a stinger-like structure. In doing so, she kills the embryo inside the egg. No butterfly caterpillar will hatch from it now. Fewer caterpillars means fewer leaves will be eaten. The mustard plants will be protected.

But the female wasp doesn't simply destroy the butterfly eggs she finds. She uses them as small safe places in which to lay her own eggs. Tiny wasps will hatch from those eggs. Someday, when they're grown, these wasps may catch the scent of black mustard plants in trouble. They will respond like their mothers did and become plant bodyguards too.

THE SCIENCE BEHIND THE STORY

Plants can't hide from predators. They can't fly or run away. Even so, plants are far from defenseless. Black mustard plants produce substances that make their leaves taste bad to most plant eaters. But cabbage white caterpillars actually like the taste of mustard leaves. So when cabbage white butterflies mount an egg-laying attack, mustard plants fight back by getting wasps to defend them.

German biologist Nina Fatouros studies black mustard plants and their wasp bodyguards. Working with colleagues at Wageningen University and the Netherlands Institute of Ecology, Fatouros carried out experiments to better understand how this defense system works. The scientists put two mustard plants in closed containers. One plant had just-laid large cabbage white butterfly eggs on its leaves. The other plant was egg-free. The researchers then added a Y-shaped tunnel to their experimental setup. One arm of the Y led to the egg-free plant. The other arm led to the plant with eggs.

Periodically the scientists released tiny wasps into the tunnel, at the bottom of the Y. They recorded whether the wasps flew up one arm or the other—or stayed put. "We tested three different time points," Fatouros explained. "We saw a response after 24 hours."

At first, the wasps didn't do much of anything. But after twenty-four hours, they purposefully headed down the arm of the Y leading to the egg-infested plant. The experiment showed that the wasps were attracted by a chemical scent—Fatouros calls such scents "volatiles"—released by egg-infested mustard plants. The scent is like a cry for help.

Once the wasps arrived, they started laying eggs. "The female wasp kills the butterfly egg when she lays her egg inside it," said Fatouros. No butterfly eggs, no destructive caterpillars. "I think it's remarkable that a plant with no brain and that cannot run away is able to make use of animals to defend itself."

When it comes to animal (and plant!) defenses, nature seems to have no shortage of remarkable strategies. Scientists regularly discover new defenses that are more clever and more amazing than anything video game developers will ever dream up. In the survival game that is life, living things display endlessly creative ways to outsmart and outmaneuver whatever wants to eat them.

A large cabbage white butterfly prepares to lay her eggs on a black mustard plant leaf. The plant will continue to summon its tiny wasp bodyguards until the threat from the butterflies has passed.

A NOTE FROM THE AUTHOR

Writing books is hard work. So is doing science. But both are also fun because they involve real discovery and lots of surprises. I could never have written this book without the help of the scientists featured in these pages, and their willingness to share their time and insights. Many thanks to Douglas Fudge, David Blackburn, Egon Heiss, Thomas Bourguignon, Sheila Patek, Wade Sherbrooke, Robert Young, and Nina Fatouros—I love that you love your work as much as I do mine.

SOURCE NOTES

8 Douglas Fudge, personal communication with the author, December 7, 2013.
8 Ibid.
9 Ibid.
9 Ibid.
12 David Blackburn, personal communication with the author, November 22, 2013.
13 Ibid.
13 Ibid.
13 Ibid.
14 Egon Heiss, personal communication with the author, November 25, 2013.
15 Ibid.
18 Thomas Bourguignon, personal communication with the author, November 17, 2013.
19 Ibid.
30 Sheila Patek, "(Un)Silent Sea," University of Massachusetts Honors 291A Faculty Lectures—Fall 2012, accessed November 12, 2013, https://www.honors.umass.edu/honors-faculty-lectures.
31 Sheila Patek, personal communication with the author, November 14, 2013.
31 Ibid.
35 Wade Sherbrooke, personal communication with the author, November 13, 2013.
35 Ibid.
35 Ibid.
38 Robert Young, personal communication with the author, November 5, 2013.
39 Ibid.
39 Ibid.
43 Nina Fatouros, personal communication with the author, November 8, 2013.
43 Ibid.
43 Ibid.

GLOSSARY

amphibian: a cold-blooded, vertebrate animal that begins life as a water-dwelling form with gills but develops into an air-breathing adult with lungs. Frogs and salamanders are amphibians.

bacteria: extremely small, single-celled living things. Just one is called a bacterium.

camouflage: patterns, coloring, body structures, and other features that help animals blend into their surroundings and go unnoticed by predators

carcass: the dead body of an animal

contract: to shorten quickly. When muscles contract, they shorten and pull on structures they are attached to.

deploy: to put into action; to use

evolution: gradual change in living things over time

feces: solid or semisolid animal wastes; excrement; poop

gills: organs used by water-dwelling animals such as fish to extract oxygen from water for respiration (breathing)

gland: a structure or organ in an animal or plant that produces and releases one or more chemical substances

instinct: a natural tendency to behave in a particular way. To do something instinctively is to act based on instinct.

keratin: a tough protein found in hair, nails, hooves, claws, and other animal body parts

mandibles: jaws or jaw-like mouthparts used for grabbing and biting

mucus: a slippery, somewhat thick, usually clear substance produced by glands or cells

predator: an animal that eats other animals for food

prey: an animal eaten by a predator

salamander: an amphibian with four legs, an elongated body, a tail, and large bulging eyes

salivary: relating to saliva, which is a clear, watery substance produced by glands in an animal's mouth involved in digesting food

species: a particular type of living thing

toxic: poisonous

turbine: a machine used to generate electricity that has spinning blades set in motion by a fast-moving flow of water, air, or steam

vertebrate: an animal with a backbone and a skeleton made of bone or cartilage

SELECTED BIBLIOGRAPHY

Blackburn, David C., James Hanken, and Farish A. Jenkins, Jr. "Concealed Weapons: Erectile Claws in African Frogs." *Biology Letters*, 4, no. 4, (August 23, 2008): 355–357.

Fatouros, Nina E., Dani Lucas-Barbosa, Berhane T. Weldegergis, Foteini G. Pashalidou, Joop J. A. van Loon, Marcel Dicke, Jeffrey A. Harvey, Rieta Gols, and Martinus E. Huigens. "Plant Volatiles Induced by Herbivore Egg Deposition Affect Insects of Different Trophic Levels." *PLoS ONE*, August 17, 2012. doi: 10.1371/journal.pone.0043607.

Goulart, Vinícius D. L. R., and Robert J. Young. "Selfish Behaviour as an Antipredator Response in Schooling Fish?" *Animal Behaviour*, 86, no. 2, (August 2013): 443–450.

Heiss, E., N. Natchev, D. Salaberger, M. Gumpenberger, A. Rabanser, and J. Weisgram. "Hurt Yourself to Hurt Your Enemy: New Insights on the Function of the Bizarre Antipredator Mechanism in the Salamandrid *Pleurodeles waltl* (Michahelles, 1830)." *Journal of Zoology*, 280, no. 2, (February 2010): 156–162.

Negishi, A., C. L. Armstrong, L. Kreplak, M.C. Rheinstadter, L. T. Lim, T. E. Gillis, and D. S. Fudge. "The Production of Fibers and Films from Solubilized Hagfish Slime Thread Proteins." *Biomacromolecules*, 13, no. 11, (2012): 3475–3482.

Patek, S. N., M. V. Rosario, and J. R. A. Taylor. "Comparative Spring Mechanics in Mantis Shrimp." *Journal of Experimental Biology*, 216, (April 1, 2013): 1317–1329.

Sherbrooke, Wade C., Andrew Mitchell, Kelly Sweet, Linda Searles, and Darlene Braastad. "Negative Oral Responses of a Non-Canid Mammalian Predator (Bobcat, *Lynx rufus*; Felidae) to Ocular-Sinus Blood-Squirting of Texas and Regal Horned Lizards, *Phrynosoma cornutum* and *Phrynosoma solare*." *Herpetological Review*, 43, no. 3, (2012): 386–391.

Šobotník, J., T. Bourguignon, R. Hanus, Z. Demianová, J. Pytelková, M. Mareš, P. Foltynová, J. Preisler, J. Cvačka, J. Krasulová, and Y. Roisin. "Explosive Backpacks in Old Termite Workers." *Science*, 337, no. 6093, (July 27, 2012): 436.

MORE TO EXPLORE

BOOKS

Jenkins, Steve. *The Animal Book: A Collection of the Fastest, Fiercest, Toughest, Cleverest, Shyest—and Most Surprising—Animals on Earth.* New York: HMH Books for Young Readers, 2013. This book is full of startling facts and creative illustrations about more than three hundred animals.

Johnson, Rebecca L. *Zombie Makers: True Stories of Nature's Undead.* Minneapolis: Millbrook Press, 2013. Can't get enough of bizarre animal behavior? Check out how some animals can control the minds—and bodies—of other animals.

Sherbrooke, Wade C. *Introduction to Horned Lizards of North America.* Berkeley: University of California Press, 2003. Wade Sherbrooke literally wrote the book about horned lizards. You'll find everything you want to know about these amazing animals in this well-illustrated guide.

WEBSITES

Bugs in the Picture
http://www.bugsinthepicture.com
Many scientists are also great photographers. Get a closeup look at some amazing insects—including butterfly-egg-killing wasps—at this site created by biologist Nina Fatouros and her colleagues.

Comparative Biomaterials Lab
www.comparativephys.ca/members/dfudge
This is the website for Douglas Fudge's laboratory at the University of Guelph, where you can explore what's going on in his laboratory and what new discoveries about hagfish—and other creatures—he and his students are making.

Dr. David Blackburn
www.calacademy.org/science/heroes/dblackburn/
Learn about David Blackburn's love of frogs and the amazing adventures he has had studying them in different parts of the world. And don't miss the song "7000 Amphibians" at http://www.calacademy.org/sciencetoday/7000-kinds-of-amphibians.

Stomatopods
http://arthropoda.southernfriedscience.com/?cat=34
Explore the posts under the heading Stomatopods for fascinating stories and facts about mantis shrimp.

The Patek Lab
www.thepateklab.org
See photos, watch videos, and read about the research on mantis shrimp and other cool animals studied by Sheila Patek and her students at Duke University.

VIDEOS

"Exploding Termites Defend Their Colony"
http://www.youtube.com/watch?v=xecJSrseQcU
See a blue-spotted *N. taracua* termite detonate her chemical defense system—in slow-motion!—while under attack by enemy termites.

"Fooled by Nature: Fulmar Chick's Vomit"
http://science.howstuffworks.com/zoology/28383-fooled-by-nature-fulmar-chicks-vomit-video.htm
This vivid video of a fulmar chick in action will help you appreciate just how good it is at defending itself.

"Hagfish Slime"
http://www.youtube.com/watch?v=pmaal7Hf0WA
This brief video clip shows close-up views of how and how fast a hagfish deploys its slimy defense.

"Hagfish Slime Defense Mechanism"
http://www.youtube.com/watch?v=pfyq4Zhr5Y8&noredirect=1#t=14
Watch deep-sea video footage of a hagfish defending itself with slime against predators!

"Speed Kills: The Fastest Punch in the World"
http://www.youtube.com/watch?v=DtNAqK_V-lg
Video and animations show the details of a mantis shrimp's astonishing punch.

"High Speed Video of a Mantis Shrimp Striking a Snail Shell"
http://www.youtube.com/watch?v=ZTyFrYhpc1Y
Watch a mantis shrimp strike a snail in a video clip slowed down to a fraction of actual speed.

INDEX

PHOTO ACKNOWLEDGMENTS

The images in this book are used with the permission of: © Jamen Percy/Shutterstock.com (blood drips); © Lukiyanova Natalia/frenta/Shutterstock.com, p. 4; © Martin Harvey/Gallo Images/CORBIS, p. 5; © Mark Conlin/SuperStock/Corbis, p. 6; Courtesy of the National Museum of New Zealand Te Papa Tongarewa, p. 7 (all); © Mathew McCarthy/Waterloo Region Record, p. 9; © Daniel Portik/Museum of Vertebrate Zoology/University of California Berkeley, p. 10; © Pat De La Harpe/naturepl.com, p. 11; © David C. Blackburn, Ph.D., pp. 12, 13; © age fotostock /Alamy, p. 14; © Egon Heiss, University of Vienna, p. 15; © Dr. Robert Hanus, pp. 16, 17 (all); © J. Sobotnik, p. 18; © blickwinkel/Kaminski/Alamy, p. 20; © Zoonar RF/Thinkstock, p. 21 (left); © FLPA/Alamy, p. 21 (right); © mcb bank bhalwal/Flickr/Getty Images, p. 22; © Mike Powles /Oxford Scientific/Getty Images, p. 23; © Mike Lane/Alamy, p. 24 (top); © Annelies Leeuw, p. 24 (bottom); © Chris Newbert/Minden Pictures/CORBIS, p. 26; © Christopher Crowley /Visuals Unlimited, Inc. p. 27; © Roy Caldwell, pp. 28-29, 30, 31 (right); © Jon Gardiner/Duke Photography, p.31 (left); © NHPA/SuperStock, p. 32; © Michael Quinton/Minden Pictures /CORBIS, p. 33; © National Geographic Creative, p. 34; © Raymond Mendez/Animals Animals, p. 35; © JJPhoto.dk, pp. 36, 37, 39; © Walter Bibikow/age fotostock/Getty Images, p. 40; © Dr. Nina E. Fatouros/Wageningen University, p. 41; © GIPhotoStock RF/Alamy, p. 42; © Tibor Bukovinszky, p. 43.

Front cover: © Roy Caldwell.